Saints of North America

by
Jean Olwen Maynard

*All booklets are published thanks to the
generous support of the members of the
Catholic Truth Society*

CATHOLIC TRUTH SOCIETY
PUBLISHERS TO THE HOLY SEE

Contents

All rights reserved. First published 2017 by The Incorporated Catholic Truth Society, 40-46 Harleyford Road, London SE11 5AY Tel: 020 7640 0042 Fax: 020 7640 0046. © 2017 The Incorporated Catholic Truth Society.

ISBN 978 1 78469 170 7

Encounters

In 1534 Jacques Cartier sailed into the Gulf of St Lawrence, set up a tall cross on the seashore, and claimed the land for France. In a second voyage he sailed up the St Lawrence River as far as a large island, crowned with a mountain which he named "Mount Royal" (Montreal). Coming across a large indigenous settlement, he asked the name of the place and was told "kanata" (meaning "village"): that is how the country came to be called Canada. The French colony there, which would also be known as New France, began with Samuel de Champlain, who founded Quebec in 1608, and formed alliances with the neighbouring indigenous peoples: the Algonquins and Montagnards, and the Wendat Confederacy whom the French knew as the Hurons. They, as well as the French, stood to make substantial profits from the fur trade, particularly the supply of beaver pelts, which were in high demand in Europe for hat manufacture. But Champlain also helped his allies militarily, providing them with weapons, and siding with them against the Five Nations of the Iroquois Confederacy to the south. This set off a war which was to last for most of the seventeenth century.

The first English colony – Jamestown, Virginia – was established in 1607, and in 1620 the Pilgrim Fathers arrived in the Mayflower to settle in what would become New England. The Dutch set up a fur trading post on the Hudson River, which they named Fort Orange, and in 1625 founded New Amsterdam on Manhattan Island. Forming an alliance with the Iroquois – in particular the Mohawks, who were the most powerful of the Five Nations – the Dutch kept them well supplied with guns, and were only too glad to support them against the French and their allies, who were rivals of the Dutch and the Iroquois in the fur trade.

The various colonising initiatives usually cited, as part of their purpose and justification, the propagation of Christianity among the peoples of the new world, but this was clearly not their driving motivation. Nevertheless Champlain, a devout Catholic, took it more seriously than most, and made a point of inviting missionaries to come over and do something about it.

The Gospel in New France

A party of five Jesuits – three priests and two lay brothers – arrived in Quebec in 1625, and the youngest of the priests, Fr Jean (John) de Brébeuf, set off as soon as possible to spend some months living with a First Nation community. It involved huge hardships – constantly moving from place to place, sleeping in his host family's crowded, smoke-filled cabin, and shivering through the winter snow, when all too often there was not enough food, and everyone went hungry. Moreover he was unable to make even a single convert. Nevertheless he stuck with it, and wouldn't give up. The Hurons could not pronounce his surname, so called him "Echon", which was their way of saying "John". He became an expert on the Huron language and culture, and as more Jesuit missionaries arrived – priests, brothers, and lay volunteers called *donnés* – they were sent to him for training. Among them was Fr Isaac Jogues, who had offered himself for the missions shortly after his ordination in January 1636, and arrived that summer. Some of the Hurons were beginning to convert to Christianity, but by then their very existence as a people was under threat.

The indigenous nations had no immunity to European germs. A smallpox epidemic just a few years previously had wiped out over half their populations; now an outbreak of influenza claimed more lives. In both the Iroquois and the Huron cultures, dealing with bereavement was taken very seriously, and traditionally one of their ways of doing it was to go to war, to work off their grief and acquire replacement people through capture. Despite their catastrophic losses, the Iroquois were still a formidable fighting force, and the Hurons got the worst of it. As they listened to what the Jesuits were saying, the big question that exercised their minds was: could these "black robes" offer something which might save them from the sickness and the Iroquois raiding parties – or were they malicious sorcerers who were deliberately causing these disasters?

"Holy maidens"

Meanwhile a pioneer missionary of a completely different kind arrived on the scene. Marie Guyart had grown up in the French city of Tours. At the age of seven she had a dream in which Jesus Christ bent down to her, asking, "Do you want to be mine?" "Yes!" she replied. She married at seventeen, but her husband's business failed, and he died two years later. This was in 1619: Marie was left a widow with a six month old baby son named Claude. People were pressing her to remarry, but she refused, and went to live with her sister and her brother-in-law, Paul Buisson.

On the eve of the Feast of the Annunciation in 1620 she had a vision in which all her sins and weaknesses were revealed to her with complete clarity, yet at the same time she saw herself bathed in the Blood of Christ, and felt an overwhelming sense of God's love. This marked a watershed in her life. To earn her keep she did whatever work she could, both around the house and in Paul's haulage business, which he put her in charge of. This involved (among other things) looking after thirty very rough waggoneers, and keeping them in order: no swearing was allowed at mealtimes, and if they went straight to bed after getting back from a trip, she'd wake them to make them say their prayers. Meanwhile the mystical experiences continued, making her increasingly convinced that she was called to the religious life. In 1631, when young Claude was eleven, she entered the Ursuline convent in Tours, becoming Sr Marie de l'Incarnation (Mary

of the Incarnation). The Ursulines were cloistered teaching nuns, famous for the girls' schools they ran inside their convents. She'd arranged for Claude to stay with his aunt and uncle, where he was well looked after; nevertheless he was very upset, and several times organised his schoolfriends to join him in desperate protests at the convent gates, where he would stand crying bitterly and shouting, "Give me back my mother!" It nearly broke her heart, but she was sure she'd made the right decision, and it would all work out in the end.

Reading the *Jesuit Relations* which were published each year, full of exciting stories of their missions in New France, she learned that the Jesuits were appealing for a French "lady" to come and start a school for the First Nation girls. This tied in with a dream she'd had of walking with a companion through a strange country full of mountains, so she wrote off to volunteer, and was thrilled to receive a reply from Fr Charles Garnier written on birch bark. Then a wealthy young widow, Madeleine de la Peltrie, came forward offering to fund the venture. After recruiting two other Ursulines, they all set sail across the Atlantic in 1639 to found a convent in Quebec. They gave their first, temporary, house the ironic nickname "The Louvre", because a palace it was not, but within a few years they moved into a small but solid purpose-built convent, surrounded by a high wooden enclosure. First Nation people from far and wide flocked to visit the convent: they were very curious to meet these "holy maidens" whose headdresses covered everything except their faces, and who could only be conversed with through holes in a grille. Mother Marie learned their languages, compiled dictionaries and wrote a catechism. She also recorded their traditional customs and beliefs, and their explorations of what it meant to be Christian.

Obliged in 1641 to take a break in Quebec to recover from a broken collarbone, Fr Brébeuf visited the Ursuline Convent and was deeply impressed by Mother Marie, and with the progress of the few First Nation girls whose parents had been persuaded to place them with the nuns. Those girls were admitted free of charge, whereas French boarders paid fees – in money if they had any, or else in consignments of butter, pigs and firewood. Hardly any of the indigenous girls stayed for long – they grew homesick for the freedom of the woodlands – but a great many stayed temporarily. Mother Marie's practicality and business sense stood her Ursuline community in good stead, and all the most important people in Quebec used to seek her advice – both on spiritual matters, and on problems facing the colony. Her son Claude found happiness and fulfilment as a Benedictine monk. He and his mother remained close in spirit despite being on opposite sides of the Atlantic, and frequently wrote to each other. In her letters she told him everything that was going on in New France, so they became an important source on the early history of Canada.

Fr Brébeuf also met with Paul Maisonneuve and Jeanne Mance, leaders of a group of colonists backed by the famous St Sulpice seminary in Paris, who were wintering in Quebec before proceeding to Montreal, one hundred and eighty miles up the St Lawrence, to found a settlement which would spread the gospel to the native peoples of New France. They saw Montreal as empty and unused. Unfortunately, the Iroquois saw it as part of their hunting grounds, and also as a sensitive frontier area where any permanent settlement of non-Iroquois posed a threat to their interests. An embassy they had sent to New France to propose a trading treaty had been rebuffed, and they were preparing to go on the warpath. The colonists' "Town of Mary" at Montreal would arouse them to even greater fury.

Martyrdoms

Fr Brébeuf had begun to establish fortified mission villages around the Great Lakes, each named after a saint. For his growing number of converts he wrote the "Huron Carol", Canada's oldest Christmas song, with lyrics in their language set to a French folk tune. But in August 1642 Fr Jogues and two *donnés* – Guillaume Couture and René Goupil – were travelling with a party of Christian Hurons when they were captured by a Mohawk warband. Couture had shot a Mohawk, so they pulled out his fingernails, and viciously bit his fingers and chewed them down to the bone. When Fr Jogues made an attempt to help Couture, they did the same to him. After a long forced march to the Iroquois homeland, the captives were made to run the gauntlet, past rows of angry people who jeered at and hit them, and jabbed sticks into their wounds, and a woman cut off Fr Jogues's thumb.

The Iroquois and the Hurons had very similar customs with regard to captured foes. After the initial mistreatment, a few might be selected to undergo death by sadistic torture: they were expected to endure their suffering with stoic defiance, thereby dying with honour, and winning the admiration of their torturers. But most, possibly even all of them, could hope to be adopted into their captors' community, provided they were willing to abandon their previous identities, and co-operate wholeheartedly in being reinvented as Iroquois. Couture quickly won acceptance, but the tribal elders could not reach consensus about Fr Jogues and Goupil: the majority favoured their adoption, but an intransigent traditionalist faction said no. While their fate remained undecided, they were held at Ossernenon, the easternmost Mohawk settlement about fifty miles from Fort Orange, treated as slaves and kept on short rations. A Mohawk warrior who saw Goupil making the sign of the cross over the village children, thinking he was casting a spell, killed him with a tomahawk. After about ten months, the half-starved Fr Jogues was rescued by the kind intervention of the Dutch Protestants of Fort Orange: they paid a ransom to the Mohawks, and gave him money to travel to New Amsterdam where he took a ship to France.

The mutilation of his hands should have disqualified Fr Jogues from celebrating Mass, but the Pope gave him a special dispensation. Much to his embarrassment, he was made a celebrity of in France as a "living martyr", but as soon as possible he returned to Canada. His greatest desire was to take the message of salvation to the Mohawks who'd tortured him. In 1645 an exchange of prisoners between the Iroquois and the French brought Guillaume Couture back to New France, as part of an Iroquois delegation charged with negotiating a peace agreement, and in 1646 Fr Jogues travelled to Ossernenon with a *donné*, Jean de Lalande. But the fractiousness of intra-Mohawk politics hadn't changed. On 18th October Fr Jogues was summoned to a longhouse where a conference was under way. As he entered, a young warrior intervened to try to protect him but was violently knocked aside, and the Jesuit was dispatched with a tomahawk. Lalande was killed the following day.

The Iroquois traditionalists achieved their goal of reigniting the war, and raids into Huron territory resumed with renewed fury. On 4th July 1648 Fr Antoine Daniel was celebrating an early Mass at the mission village of St Joseph when the Iroquois made a surprise dawn attack. He hurriedly gave general absolution and baptised the catechumens, then left the church and walked towards the raiders carrying a cross. They shot him full of arrows, threw his body into the chapel and set fire to it. During the course of that year the Dutch stepped up the supply of guns to their native allies, and as winter set in, a thousand well-armed warriors descended on the Hurons. The mission of St Ignace fell during the early hours of 16th March 1649. Three wounded survivors fled to St Louis, where they found Fr Brébeuf and Fr Gabriel Lalement, and warned them that the Iroquois were close behind. The priests helped with the evacuation, sending the women, children and elderly out of the gates to hide in the forest. Stephen Annaotaha, a devoutly Christian war chief, told them to go too, but they insisted on staying with the defenders, administering Baptism or absolution to them as they fell. Eventually Annaotaha and about sixty warriors were captured, along with the Jesuits, and they were dragged off to the ruins of St Ignace where they were made to run the gauntlet.

Next came a conference: the Iroquois needed to decide which of the captives to take home for adoption, and which to kill. A senior warrior argued strongly in favour of keeping the Jesuits alive to be held for ransom. To add emphasis to his words, he presented two necklaces of wampum: these were valuable ceremonial items, made of treasured shell beads. But at that point a former Huron who had been one of Fr Brébeuf's converts, but was now an Iroquois, chose to intervene. Perhaps his experiences had led him to become bitterly disillusioned with Christianity, or perhaps the best way he felt able to affirm his new identity was to reject and mock the faith he had once embraced. "Echon," he cried, "You say that Baptism and the suffering of this life lead straight to Paradise. You will go there soon, for I am going to baptise you and make you suffer well." So saying, he picked up the kettle hanging over the fire, and poured the boiling water three times over the priest's head. This settled the matter: both Jesuits were bound to stakes and tortured to death. Fr Brébeuf died that afternoon, Fr Lalement the following morning. The Iroquois cut out their hearts and ate them, hoping thereby to acquire a share of the amazing courage they had shown.

Frs Charles Garnier and Noël Chabanel were working together at the mission village of St Jean, serving the Petun people who were allied to the Hurons. There was no way of knowing where the Iroquois would strike next. The Jesuits didn't want to abandon their flocks, but also didn't want to risk losing two priests, so early in December 1649 Fr Chabanel, the younger of the two, was ordered to move to a safer location. He set off with a travelling party of laypeople who had also decided to leave. On 7th December the Iroquois attacked St Jean. Fr Garnier ran from cabin to cabin, baptising and giving absolution, until struck by a bullet in the chest and another in the thigh; though mortally wounded, he crawled across to another wounded man to give absolution before he died. The next day Fr Chabanel's party heard shouts from behind them, and quickly scattered into the forest, fearing that the Iroquois were on their trail. Fr Chabanel was left alone with Louis Honareenhax, a Huron who had converted to Christianity but then turned against the faith because he reckoned it had brought him bad luck. Honareenhax had developed a hatred of the Jesuits, and he took the opportunity to raise his tomahawk and bring it down on Fr Chabanel's head. He then pillaged his belongings, threw the body into the river, and later boasted of what he'd done.

The eight North American Martyrs were canonised in 1930. They are honoured at two major shrines: in Auriesville, New York State (USA), and in Midland, Ontario (Canada).

Holy Martyrs of North America, protect with your prayers the continent which was blessed by the shedding of your blood, that the Christian faith may flourish there in freedom, and its nations be a force for good throughout the world. We ask this through Jesus Christ our Lord. Amen.

The state of life of the journeying Virgin Mary

At the age of twenty, Marguerite Bourgeoys had joined what she called "the Congregation". The Congregation de Notre Dame (Congregation of Our Lady) was an order of strictly enclosed nuns who ran a prestigious girls' boarding school in their convent in Troyes, in the Champagne region of France. However Marguerite was not a nun: she belonged to a group of laywomen attached to the Congregation, whose members lived lives of prayer and charity in the world, and ran a day school for poor children. She was quickly entrusted with a leadership role, which she held for the next twelve years. Nevertheless, she felt God was calling her to something more. She wanted very much to be allowed to take religious vows, but Church regulations at the time required all women religious to be enclosed. The options, as her spiritual director saw it, were to be a contemplative like Mary of Bethany in the Gospels, or follow an active apostolate like Martha – only within the cloister, like the Ursulines or the Congregation nuns. But he agreed with her that there ought to be a third option: "the state of life of the journeying Virgin Mary, which must also be honoured, was not yet filled."

The nun charged with looking after the lay group, Sr Louise, often talked to them about her intrepid brother Maisonneuve, and his Town of Mary in Montreal, and they were thrilled when, in 1652, the man himself arrived on a visit. He was on the lookout to recruit more *habitants* (settlers), and in particular he needed a woman teacher. Marguerite was willing to volunteer, and the following year set off with him for Canada. As it turned out, no prospective schoolchildren were waiting for her in Montreal: conditions were so hard that for eight years not a single baby survived infancy. But that didn't matter: she was living the vocation to which she felt God was calling her, fully dedicated to his service, yet out in the world, responding to other people's needs – practical or spiritual – as and how they arose. She took responsibility for several young girls who seemed to have no one to look after them. The habitants had developed a custom of making devotional pilgrimages to the cross planted by Maisonneuve on top of Mount Royal, but Iroquois attacks made this too dangerous, so she organised the building of a pilgrimage chapel a little way outside the settlement, to be dedicated to Notre Dame de Bon Secours (Our Lady of Good Help). Always, in the midst of her hard work, her greatest contribution was to inspire cheerfulness and courage, and an unfailing hope in God.

Four years after her arrival, there were enough children to make it worth starting a school, and Maisonneuve gave her a former stable in which to do it. The children helped her clean up the building, and she, they and the other teachers slept up in the loft, being careful to pull up the ladder each night for fear of marauders. It was in the stable school that, together with a few companions, Marguerite started her new religious community which became the Congregation de Notre Dame de Montreal. Unusually, no dowries were required, so any young woman was welcome to join, however poor her family. So as to be self-supporting, the Sisters had a farm nearby, and the buildings there were used to accommodate unaccompanied girls sent out from France as prospective brides for the colonists.

The Congregation ran classes for poor habitant girls in domestic science; training workshops to enable young women to earn their living through spinning, weaving and needlework; small schools in outlying settlements; and a school and mission for the Hurons.

Appointment of a bishop

Canada clearly needed its own bishop, but a huge row was raging in France about how to organise it and whom to appoint. Mother Marie de l'Incarnation had written to Claude that nobody in Quebec expected a decision to be made in 1659, but then suddenly, without any warning, a ship arrived bringing the new bishop: François (Francis)  de Laval. Though only thirty-five, he came from an ancient noble family, and at once began throwing his weight around, determined to assert his authority. Mother Marie was impressed by his plain speaking and his refusal to defer to public opinion, but arguably he was far too blunt, heavy handed and provocative: the Jesuits certainly thought so, and were sure the bickering between him and the Governor of New France would end in violence.

Yet the bishop showed no sign of any personal pride or animus. Whenever a battle was ended, whether he'd won or lost, he was happy to let bygones be bygones. On some issues he was definitely in the right – for example, in striving to ban the supply of brandy to First Nation people, because they couldn't handle it, their communities were being torn apart by drunken violence, and their own leaders wanted a ban. His lifestyle was extraordinarily modest. He got up at three o'clock each morning, and spent several hours praying before the Blessed Sacrament. In between pastoral visits and administrative duties he did voluntary service at Quebec's "Hotel-Dieu" ("God's hotel", a hospital caring for the sick poor), making beds and nursing the sick. Although he had hardly any money, he gave most of it away. In the name of unity, good order and economy, he proposed merging the Quebec Ursulines with the Congregation in Montreal, and drastic changes to their rules. But when their respective mother foundresses dug their heels in, he proved willing to listen and reconsider his idea.

In February 1663 Canada was hit by a series of major earthquakes. In the aftermath a Confraternity of the Holy Family was started to provide spiritual support for family life in Canada: Bishop Laval and Mother Marguerite played a crucial role in popularising and spreading it throughout the colony. Bishop Laval also established a seminary, so Canada could begin training its own priests.

Mission to the Iroquois

The leading fur traders in Quebec had always tended to discourage immigration from France, so as not to have to share the profits of the fur trade. Thus, when Bishop Laval first arrived, the French population was only about two thousand, not enough to defend the colony from attack, whereas the population of the thirteen English colonies, a little further south, was more like one hundred thousand. However King Louis XIV now recognised the need to provide military protection, and promote settlement. In 1664 the Iroquois lost their Dutch allies when their colony was seized by the English: New Amsterdam was renamed New York, and Fort Orange became Albany. This left them vulnerable, and in 1666 the Hurons and Algoquins, accompanied by French troops, launched an invasion of their homeland. Ossernenon, where Fr Jogues and his assistants were killed, had been abandoned: the Mohawks relocated their villages from time to time, as part of a traditional strategy for sustainable management of natural resources, and the easternmost settlement was now called Caughnawaga. The French and their allies arrived to find nobody at home: the villagers had been warned, and were all hiding in the forest. Among them was a ten year-old girl whose parents had died in a smallpox epidemic a few years previously: her father had been a Mohawk chief, and her mother an Algonquin Catholic who was captured in a raid, and adopted into the tribe. She herself had had the smallpox but recovered, though she was left horribly scarred, and with damaged eyesight: her name, Tekakwitha, is thought to mean "she bumps into things".

After burning the houses and destroying the crops in the fields, the invaders moved on to do the same to the next village along, laying waste the Iroquois territory and claiming it for France. They then withdrew, and returned to Canada. The Iroquois had suffered a major blow: the villages would have to be rebuilt, there would be less to eat for the next few months, and vulnerable members of the community would not make it through the winter. Their need to make peace with the French was self-evident: if they delayed too long, other enemy tribes would attack from the south, and they'd face a war on two fronts. Accordingly, in the summer of 1667, they sent a delegation to Quebec to discuss terms. The French insisted that if they wanted an alliance they must accept Catholic missionaries, and so the delegates returned home accompanied by three Jesuits.

Caughnawaga had been rebuilt on a new site north of the Mohawk River: it comprised about two dozen longhouses constructed of bark over a timber frame, within a stockade. A chapel was opened there, and the villagers came to pray and listen politely, but showed no interest in being baptised. Meanwhile, however, groups of Iroquois took advantage of the peace to travel to the St Lawrence, to explore opportunities for hunting and trading. Some chose to stay at the Jesuit mission of La Prairie near Montreal, where they began to engage seriously with what the priests were trying to tell them. At Baptism they were given saints' names in addition to their existing names, and often started wearing a crucifix or rosary to show they were now Christians. Thus an Iroquois Christian community began to emerge – one in which lay leaders played a key role, with Iroquois converts being largely evangelised and catechised by other Iroquois. When making visits to their home villages, these Christian Iroquois talked about their newfound faith, and from around 1672 the missionaries stationed in the Iroquois territory, much to their surprise, also began to receive requests for Baptism. A mass movement into Christianity had begun, and they could only thank God for it. But other Mohawks resented this new trend, and wanted to explore the alternative opportunities opened up by the new alliance which the Five Nations were now forging with the English.

The letters of Mother Marie de l'Incarnation reveal her hopes and prayers that the future of North America would be French, and therefore Catholic. She died on 30th April 1672, happily aware that French explorers and fur trappers, and intrepid Jesuit missionaries, were travelling further and further into the North American interior round the back of the English colonies, as part of a government policy to encircle and contain them. Her first biography was written by her son. Her spiritual daughters, the Ursulines of the Canadian Union, spread throughout Canada, and more recently to other parts of the Americas and to Asia. Marie de l'Incarnation was canonised in 2014.

St Marie Guyart de l'Incarnation, having chosen to belong to Jesus Christ, you faithfully followed his guidance. Help us, by your example and intercession, to discern his leading in our own lives, and respond with generosity and trust. We ask this through Jesus Christ, our Lord. Amen.

Lily of the Mohawks

The blanket Tekakwitha wore as her outer garment was usually draped so as to cover her head, because direct sunlight hurt her eyes, but she had grown into a confident, hard-working and highly skilled young woman. She was constantly busy, either with traditional handicrafts, or digging and planting in the fields with the other women. In the spring of 1675 she hurt her foot and could not go out, so when a visiting Jesuit happened to call at her longhouse, she was the only one there to offer hospitality and refreshments. Fr Lamberville invited her to come to the chapel once her foot got better. She said she'd like to, though she was worried that this might upset her uncle, who was hostile to Christian ideas. Her longhouse's clan mother, Anastasia Tegonhatsiongo, and an older "sister" (an adoptive sister, probably a cousin), had already migrated to La Prairie. Every departure weakened the longhouse, and understandably he didn't want to lose more people. Nevertheless Tekakwitha did start attending prayers, and she was baptised on Easter Sunday 1676, taking the name Catherine which the Mohawks pronounced as "Kateri".

That year the Jesuits moved the First Nation Christians at La Prairie to a separate settlement at Kahnawake, further up the St Lawrence, and at a safer distance from the French liquor traders in Montreal. Meanwhile, back in Caughnawaga, Tekakwitha's life was becoming increasingly difficult. Living as a Christian in a longhouse from which the other Christians had mostly moved away put her in an invidious position. The rest of the family, in their desperation not to lose her, too, behaved counter productively as families often do – harassing her dreadfully, to discourage her and make her give up this Christianity idea. When she refused to work on Sundays, they gave her no food all day. So when, in the autumn of 1677, her older "sister" sent her husband to tell her to come and join them at Kahnawake, it was hardly surprising that she took the chance to escape.

After a long and difficult journey, Tekakwitha arrived at Kahnawake. She moved into Tegonhatsiongo's longhouse, and the clan mother became an important mentor for her as she settled into this new community. She also formed a strong friendship with a young widow named Marie-Thérèse Tegaiaguenta. Tekakwitha joined in all the hard work in the fields, alongside the other women, and the bringing in of heavy bundles of firewood. But as winter closed in she spent as much time as she could in the little church, praying, although it was bitterly cold in there. She prayed particularly for her friends and relatives back home. Mass was said twice each day, and Tekakwitha was always there for both masses. At Christmas she received Holy Communion for the first time. Soon afterwards she joined a hunting party that was going out. The task of the women was to skin and preserve the meat. Everyone in the group was Christian, and common prayers were held in the morning and evening, but she missed not being able to go to Mass, and decided that even if it meant going short of food, she would never go on another hunting trip. She and Tegaiaguenta engaged in ascetic practices, something very much in line with Mohawk culture, in which the capacity to endure pain was highly honoured. Tekakwitha was also determined not to get married, though this posed serious practical difficulties due to the mutual interdependence of men's and women's work in the Mohawk way of life.

Over the next few years everyone at Kahnawake, laypeople and priests, came to think very highly of Tekakwitha, and of the gentle holiness of her life. They often came to her for advice. Her health was failing, and she was increasingly confined to her sleeping shelf, suffering from blinding headaches and fever, but she never lost her sense of joy. She died on 17th April 1680, aged only twenty-four. A few moments after her death her face, which had always been disfigured by the marks of smallpox, took on an unearthly beauty. The Jesuits, and the habitants living round about, began visiting her grave to pray to her, asking for her intercession, and reports circulated of miraculous cures and escape from disasters. She was canonised in 2012.

St Kateri Tekakwitha, in your life God revealed the beauty of his love and truth. Through your intercession may peoples of every tribe, tongue and nation, having been gathered into his Church, proclaim his greatness in one song of praise. We ask this in Jesus's name. Amen.

Legacies of love

By 1688, as far as was possible given the sparse resources available, Bishop François de Laval had created a proper Church structure for New France. He'd resolved to resign and retire at sixty-five, and had selected as his successor Jean-Baptiste de Saint-Vallier, realising too late that he was a bad choice: the man was well meaning, and a workaholic, but rigid and inflexible. For the rest of his life the "former bishop" Laval lived quietly in the seminary. He had to watch helplessly as Bishop Saint-Vallier charged round putting people's backs up, making inappropriate and insensitive changes, and doing serious damage. Nevertheless he was careful not to interfere, and did his best to keep the peace, and persuade everyone to accept his successor's authority and make the best of things.

The Congregation de Notre Dame de Montreal had grown steadily. New recruits came from France, others from habitant families in Canada, and the first Huron member, Sr Marie Thérèse Gannensagouas, entered in 1681. Mother Marguerite resolved to step down as superior in 1683, but agreed to continue in office after a disastrous fire destroyed the convent, and caused the deaths of the two Sisters best suited to take over. Not until 1693 was she able to resign, and Sr Marie Barbier was then elected superior. Bishop Saint-Vallier had always been very impressed with the work of the Congregation, and had helped the Sisters open a house in Quebec. But to Mother Barbier's horror, he started pressurising her to accept a whole set of heavy rules, under which they would become strictly enclosed, and no longer allowed to accept novices without a dowry. She appealed for help to the Sulpicians (the priests trained at St Sulpice) in Paris, and at their request, Mother Marguerite set down in writing her account of the founding charism of the community. This helped in negotiating a compromise: some of Bishop Saint-Vallier's stipulations had to be accepted, but the Congregation at long last received official recognition by the Church. To her great joy, Mother Marguerite was able to make her religious profession along with the others in 1698.

After devoting the next two years to quiet prayer, she asked God to allow her to die in place of a young nun who was dangerously ill: sure enough, the young nun recovered, and she became ill instead. She died on 12th January 1700, a few months short of her eightieth birthday. Whereas the original Congregation in Troyes did not survive the French Revolution, the Congregation de Notre Dame de Montreal continues to flourish, with branches in many parts of the world. Marguerite Bourgeoys was canonised by Pope John Paul II in 1980.

> *St Marguerite Bourgeoys, by your example and intercession may God make us ready to respond lovingly to the needs of others as they arise. We ask your prayers for our families, and for the wellbeing and happiness of all families everywhere, through Jesus Christ our Lord. Amen.*

In 1700 Bishop Saint-Vallier had to make a trip to France to sort out some ecclesiastical matters, and on the way back was captured by the English, who were at war with France, and held as a hostage. In his absence, Bishop Laval deputised, performing all the episcopal functions up to his death on 6th May 1708. As his body lay in state in Quebec Cathedral, the people flocked to pay their respects, touching their rosaries and prayer books to his body, and cutting off pieces of his robes to keep as relics. He was canonised in 2014.

St François de Laval, first pastor of the Church in Canada, through your example and intercession may we be given grace to stand up fearlessly for what is right when it is our duty to do so, and patience to accept what we can't change. We ask this through Jesus Christ our Lord. Amen.

Grey Nuns

All the best people in Montreal attended the wedding of François d'Youville and Marguerite Dufrost in 1722: their union looked like a fairy tale come true. But it all went horribly wrong. The young couple lived with François' mother, who was very wealthy but very stingy, and terribly difficult to live with, and it wasn't long before Marguerite was spending long periods alone in the house with her, while her husband was away on business. It took her longer to discover the nature of that business. François was agent for the Governor of Montreal, who was using his position to make exorbitant profits in the fur trade by forcing the indigenous suppliers to accept brandy instead of money in exchange for their pelts. This was unethical and illegal, and was wrecking the regional economy. First Nation leaders and law-abiding Montreal merchants were constantly complaining, but François took no notice, so both he and Marguerite were ostracised socially. There she was, being treated as a criminal because of something she didn't agree with, but was powerless to prevent. She had five children, but three of them died: only two little boys survived.

Marguerite's formal schooling had comprised just two years with the Ursulines in Quebec, but it had given her a solid religious grounding, and she sought comfort in her faith. She joined the Confraternity of the Holy Family, and became very active in that. After the death of her mother-in-law things got even worse, because François began drinking heavily, and gambling all his mother's money away. He himself died in July 1730. Marguerite was twenty-eight, and pregnant with a sixth child who only lived five months. François had run the estate so deeply into debt that she had no choice but to renounce the inheritance: the court did, however, allow her to lease the house, and by opening a small shop on the ground floor she managed to earn a living for herself and her surviving sons, François and Charles. But where – she agonised in her loneliness – was God in all this?

The answer which came to her was to look for him among the poor. She was joined by three women who, like her, had family responsibilities but were looking for something beyond those responsibilities. They visited the sick, collected and distributed alms for those in need, and watched and prayed by the dying and dead. Marguerite also visited prisoners, and begged money from door to door to bury the bodies of executed criminals. Some years went by, both Marguerite's sons left home to study for the priesthood, and the circumstances of the other women also changed. In November 1737 she took into her house a poor elderly woman who was blind and needed care, and on 31st December the other three also moved in. Although they wanted to commit themselves to poverty, chastity and obedience, starting a new religious order required royal approval which was unlikely to be forthcoming. So they decided just to live together as a lay community, wearing plain grey clothes, and supporting themselves by their needlework and by taking in paying guests. A year later they moved to a larger house so they could look after more needy people.

Their endeavours met with a remarkable degree of public hostility. For women to take up such a radically self-sacrificial lifestyle, without even the financial and reputational protection of official government approval, was deemed by some to be quite shocking. Also, it was rumoured that the Sulpicians were planning to put them in charge of Montreal's General Hospital. This was not a hospital in the modern sense, but a refuge for elderly and disabled men with nowhere else to go. It was very run down and close to bankruptcy, but it occupied valuable real estate, and the influential and well connected expected rich pickings when it closed down. A great many townspeople who probably had no idea of the true situation were persuaded to sign a petition against any change of management, and the d'Youville family's reputation made it easy to start a whispering campaign. People began throwing stones at Marguerite and her friends in the street, and calling them the "grey sisters" – a nasty taunt because in the local slang it carried a second meaning: "tipsy nuns".

Marguerite and her companions were undeterred by the persecution. When, in 1745, their house was destroyed in a disastrous fire, Marguerite simply declared: "Up to now, we've lived a little too comfortably; from now on we shall have more in common with the poor, because we'll be living more like them." In 1747 they took over the General Hospital, cleaned it up and opened wards for elderly women and former prostitutes. Marguerite organised all kinds of in-house production and money-generating schemes, in which the inmates worked as best they could, and so managed not only to keep it solvent, but eventually to pay off all the debts. In 1755 Marguerite and her companions were recognised as a religious congregation by the Bishop of Quebec, and permitted to take vows. Officially, they became the Sisters of Charity of the General Hospital, but Marguerite designed a grey uniform with a bonnet, and they were proud to be known as the Grey Nuns.

That year a terrible smallpox epidemic swept New France, and they took in large numbers of stricken patients, both habitants and First Nation, and nursed the majority back to health. They also cared for sick soldiers and prisoners, and after 1756, when war broke out between Britain and France, rescued British soldiers captured by France's indigenous allies. After Quebec had fallen the British forces advanced on Montreal, and prepared to bombard the General Hospital which looked like part of the fortifications, but the building was saved by the intervention of a soldier who owed his life to the Sisters. The first few years of British rule were dark and terrible, with the economy devastated and food prices sky high. Hardly able to feed themselves, parents were abandoning their newborns, so Marguerite opened a foundling home. Starting a new project seemed like sheer insanity, since vast amounts of money owed to her by the French government were irrecoverable, and the General Hospital was more deeply in debt than ever. Then in 1765 the building caught fire and was burned to the ground. But nothing could shake Marguerite's conviction that God would stand by her, and her faith was vindicated: the General Hospital was rebuilt, the debts steadily paid off, and none of the Sisters' work for the poor had to be given up.

Mother Marguerite died on 23rd December 1771. From the Grey Nuns of Montreal sprang many daughter houses, and autonomous daughter congregations, to take forward their mission throughout Canada, the United States and South America. Marguerite d'Youville was canonised in 1990.

St Marguerite d'Youville, your faith in God made the impossible possible. By your example and intercession, may we be given grace to overcome the problems and griefs we face in our own lives, and be able to serve God and others in love. We ask this through Jesus Christ our Lord. Amen.

Outposts of New Spain

The takeover of South America had yielded untold riches for the Spanish state and Spanish settlers. But the southern borderlands of North America appeared less promising, so a low-cost strategy was adopted of sending in missionaries, protected by small detachments of soldiers, to gather the indigenous people together into missions. The missionaries were to teach them about the Catholic faith, but also about European farming techniques and craft skills. In the short term, this would make the missions self-supporting, and in the longer term it was expected to develop the territories economically, and improve the indigenous people's quality of life, thereby incorporating them into Spain's global empire as loyal and productive subjects. Though well intentioned, the strategy was imposed coercively and without consultation, and aroused considerable resentment, yet it was benign compared with the genocidal violence and ethnic cleansing which native Americans suffered in some other parts of North America. The process was first attempted, with mixed results, in Florida and New Mexico in the sixteenth century. Towards the end of the seventeenth century the Franciscans developed missions in Texas, and the Jesuits in Lower California, a long narrow peninsula separated from mainland Mexico by the Gulf of California. In 1700 Fr Eusebio Kino, a Jesuit from the Italian Tyrol, began exploring and mapping Arizona, and establishing missions there.

St Junípero Serra

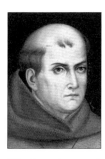

Born into a family of small farmers in Majorca in 1713, Miguel José Serra decided to join the Franciscans at seventeen, and chose the religious name "Junípero" (Juniper) after one of St Francis's early companions. Academically brilliant, he became a professor at the Llullian University in Palma, and could have spent his life there in comfort and honour, but when he was thirty-five he threw it all in to volunteer as a missionary. The reason, he said, was because his spiritual life had become stale: he wanted to get back to the "intense longings" he'd felt as a young novice. He rediscovered that early joy in the eight years he spent at missions for indigenous Pame communities in the Sierra Gorda. When he returned to Mexico City, capital of New Spain, he was much in demand as a preacher in the city churches. In 1767 the Jesuits were expelled from the Spanish Empire, and the Franciscans were asked to take over their missions. Fr Serra was put in charge of Lower California.

Upper California was still largely unexplored. Its abundant natural resources supported an indigenous hunter-gatherer population of around three hundred thousand, divided into a large number of small bands who mostly lived in peace with each other. No one knew there was gold there, yet even so, the Spanish authorities did not wish to see it taken over by another European power. The British had shown an interest, but the recently-established Russian colony in Alaska posed a more immediate threat, with Russian explorers and fur traders gradually ranging further and further down the west coast of North America. The Viceroyalty of New Spain decided it was time to move in.

By 1769 Fr Serra was fifty-six, short and asthmatic, and walked with a painful limp: a more unlikely pioneer would be difficult to imagine. Nevertheless he travelled north with the overland expedition, which was supported by ships calling at pre-agreed locations along the coast to deliver supplies. Fr Serra halted in San Diego to begin making contact with the local Kumeyaay, who initially seemed friendly but quickly turned hostile. On 15th August, when most of the soldiers were absent, they attacked. A young Mexican lay assistant took an arrow in the throat, and ran to Fr Serra who gave the last rites and comforted him as he died. "I was quite a while with him there dead," recorded Fr Serra, "and my little apartment a pool of blood. Still the exchange of shots – bullets and arrows – went on. There were only four on our side against more than twenty on theirs. And there I was with the dead man, thinking most probably I would soon have to follow him, but at the same time praying to God that the victory would be for our Catholic faith without losing a single soul." After the attack was beaten off, the soldiers built a stockade, but food stocks were dwindling, there was no sign of the supply ship, and the Spanish commander wanted to call the whole thing off and go back to Mexico. Fr Serra prayed a novena, and on the ninth day a sail appeared on the horizon.

The California missions take shape

Over the next twelve years eight more missions were founded, including San Francisco (named after St Francis of Assisi). At first the native Californians were chary of the Spanish, and the missions could not produce enough food to attract them in. The San Diego mission was destroyed in another Kumeyaay attack in November 1775, and Fr Luis Jayme beaten to death. Spanish troops scoured the surrounding countryside looking for the perpetrators, but Fr Serra wrote a passionate appeal to the authorities on their behalf. If they were found, let them be given some moderate punishment, but not put to death – and as for himself, if in future anyone should kill him, let them be forgiven.

Though the number of Spaniards and Mexicans who had travelled to California was quite small, they had unknowingly brought all kinds of germs with them,

and their herds of sheep and cattle spread out across
the countryside, impacting heavily on the local ecology.
As the native Californian communities were ravaged
by epidemics, and their natural environment lost its
capacity to sustain their traditional hunter-gatherer
lifestyle, they began moving to the missions in search
of food. As "mission Indians" they usually lived just
outside the missions, or not far off, received instruction
in the Christian faith, and worked in the mission farms
and workshops in return for their keep. They were never
forced to become Christian, but once baptised, they were
deemed to have made a commitment to settle permanently
at the mission, and were not considered free to change
their minds. If they wanted to go hunting or foraging, or
visit their non-Christian relatives, they were supposed to
seek permission, and anyone who went absent without
leave, or failed to return within a reasonable timeframe,
was liable to recapture and punishment. The way the
friars exercised their authority was definitely not a good
model of missionary outreach, but it did provide some
protection against the soldiers and the lay settlers, who
saw the mission Indians as a labour force ready to be
exploited, and who also saw the indigenous women as
theirs for the taking. Fr Serra was convinced that the
missions provided native Californians with what was
realistically their best possible option in a hard and cruel
colonial world. He was constantly on the alert to defend

them from mistreatment by the Spanish troops, and they seem to have held him in great affection.

Fr Serra had poured his heart and soul into evangelising Upper California, but when, early in 1784, a rumour spread that the missions were going to be taken away from the Franciscans and given to the Dominicans, he only said, "God's will be done. If those who come to eject us do better than we have done, we have no reason to complain." Later that year, on 27th August, he felt that his end was near, and requested the last rites, but insisted on walking to the church so he could receive them in public, and show a good example to his Californian converts. They flocked into the church, many of them crying, and some stayed with him all night. Fr Serra died peacefully the following day.

After his death the Franciscans established another twelve missions, and maintained them up to 1834 when the government of Mexico (by then independent from Spain) closed them down to free up the valuable mission lands for the increasing numbers of "Californios" (ethnically Spanish settlers). The "emancipated" native Californians were supposed to get half the land and half the livestock, but only a lucky few managed to get anything at all. Most of the land and other assets were seized by Californio ranchers, who reduced the mission Indians to peonage. Meanwhile the old mission buildings fell into ruin, but towards the end of the nineteenth century interest in them revived, and a movement began to restore and preserve them. Today they are loved and cherished as heritage centres and tourist attractions of great beauty and historical significance. Most of them are also still in Catholic ownership, and fully functioning as churches, and as beacons of faith.

Junípero Serra was canonised in 2015: he is the patron saint of California, and patron of the Serra Foundation which promotes vocations to the priesthood and religious life.

St Junípero Serra, you renounced worldly honours and comfort, your family and native land for the glory of God and the salvation of souls. Through your intercession may God draw many men and women into the priesthood and religious life. We ask this through Jesus Christ our Lord. Amen.

The Age of Revolution

An extraordinarily high proportion of the land area of North America had been claimed by France, though it was sparsely settled compared with the British colonies. In 1763 Canada, together with a broad swathe of territory between the Appalachians and the Mississippi, stretching from the Great Lakes to Florida, was ceded to Britain, and another vast area west of the Mississippi, known as Louisiana, went to Spain. To reconcile the native American peoples to British rule, King George III issued a Royal Proclamation forbidding settlers from the British colonies to acquire land west of the Appalachians. This infuriated them, and was a major factor leading to the American Revolution.

St Elizabeth Seton

Elizabeth Bayley was not yet two when, in 1776, the thirteen colonies declared independence, and formed a new nation: the United States of America. Her father was a highly dedicated New York doctor, and during the American Revolution he served as a naval surgeon – on the

British side. However this was never held against the family, and after the British defeat, they stayed on in New York. An unexpected side-effect of US independence was the disappearance of the anti-Catholic Penal Laws: this allowed the New York Catholics to begin meeting openly, and in 1786 they put up a wooden chapel on Barclay Street which they named St Peter's. But that was no concern of the Bayleys, who were respectably Episcopalian. In 1794 Elizabeth married William Seton in a fashionable ceremony at Holy Trinity Episcopal Church. They were head over heels in love, and over the next eight years their marriage was blessed with five children. In between having babies, Elizabeth found time for voluntary work: she helped set up the Society for the Relief of Poor Widows with Small Children, the first US charitable association, and served as treasurer.

Then William's business got into difficulties. Elizabeth did her best to help him, acting as his secretary and writing letters to creditors. Nevertheless he eventually went bankrupt, and then began to show symptoms of TB, which the doctor thought had been brought on by all the stress. He eventually recommended a long sea voyage. So William, Elizabeth and their eight year-old daughter Anna set off for Italy, leaving their four younger children in America. Tragically, the authorities in Tuscany were in a state of panic about reports of yellow fever in New York, and when their ship docked, in mid-winter, the Setons were allowed off only to be locked up in an unheated quarantine unit. William's trading partners, Filippo and Antonio Filicchi, did what they could to help, sending in food and blankets, and Elizabeth's uncomplaining devotion to nursing her husband won their deep admiration. But he deteriorated rapidly, and three months later he was dead.

After the funeral Elizabeth and Anna stayed for a while with the Filicchi family. Mass was celebrated daily in their domestic chapel, and Elizabeth found the presence of God in the Eucharist becoming very important to her. Eventually Antonio escorted her back to New York where, as a way of earning a living while looking after her children, she started a small fee-paying school. Shortly afterwards she asked Rev. John Hobart, the curate at Holy Trinity, to tell her more about the doctrine of the Real Presence. She was very taken aback when he gave her a heap of anti-Catholic tracts to read, and began browbeating her about letting herself be taken in by wily foreign Papists. Antonio was touring America fixing up business deals, but he kept in touch. On Ash Wednesday 1805 she plucked up her courage, and went into the Barclay Street chapel. Mass was in progress, it was full of poor, shabbily dressed immigrants, and an Irish priest was preaching a cheerful sermon about death. Elizabeth was thrilled. She was fed up with people skating politely round the idea of death, and here was someone prepared to talk about it. Even if her friends and relatives never spoke to her again, she was going to become a Catholic. She was received into the Church at St Peter's in March 1805.

As news of her conversion spread, shocked parents withdrew their daughters from her school. Antonio suggested moving to Canada, but when that idea didn't come off, he paid the boys' fees so they could be enrolled at a Catholic boarding school in Maryland. The headmaster there was Fr Louis Dubourg, one of a number of Sulpician priests who had come over as refugees from the French Revolution, and offered their services to the Bishop of Baltimore, John Carroll – the first, and at that time the only, US Catholic bishop. The USA had started off as a very large country, because in making peace at the end of the War of Independence, Britain had ceded the area between the Appalachians and the Mississippi, and in 1803 President Jefferson almost doubled the size of it again through the Louisiana Purchase, whereby the land west of the Mississippi was sold to the US for fifty million francs. In all parts of this vast country there were significant numbers of Catholics, but relatively few priests – so the Sulpician refugees played a vital role in those early years.

In 1806 Bishop Carroll visited New York and confirmed Elizabeth: they got on well and became friends. A couple of years later she got to know Fr Dubourg, when he came to New York to raise money for his boys' school, and he invited her to come to Baltimore to open a girls' school. A small house was available, her daughters could live with her, and her sons could attend his college for free.

Emmitsburg

Two other young women came to help Elizabeth, and the idea was mooted that they should form a teaching sisterhood. Founding a religious congregation requires excellent skills of leadership, and Bishop Carroll and Fr Dubourg had not, till then, been able to find anyone who seemed up to it. But Elizabeth seemed ideal. Unlike Marie Guyart, she was firmly convinced that her vocation as a mother came before anything else, but it was agreed that her parental responsibilities would be respected, and the girls could live with her in the convent. The only remaining problem was the need for a much larger house. Then an offer came up of a large farm in Emmitsburg. Elizabeth wasn't too pleased: it was out in the wilds, and she'd always been a town dweller. Nevertheless she agreed, and the nascent community moved to Emmitsburg. They adopted a costume similar to what Elizabeth had been wearing since she was widowed: a black dress with a little shoulder cape, and a white cap. Later, for practical reasons, the colour of the cap was changed to black. The early years were far from easy, with all the hard work and responsibility involved in starting a new religious congregation and boarding school on a shoestring, at the same time as looking after, and constantly worrying about, her children. But Elizabeth's biggest problems were with difficult priests.

Elizabeth got on very well with Bishop Carroll and some of the Sulpicians, but there were others who were dreadfully uptight and authoritarian. Discovering that Fr John Baptist David was planning to get her replaced by another Sister who'd be more under his thumb, she wrote to Bishop Carroll pointing out that the vows she'd taken were renewable annually, and since she hadn't renewed them, she was free to leave. What actually happened was that in 1811 Bishop Carroll was made an archbishop, whereupon he began appointing bishops for other parts of America, one of whom took Fr David off with him to Kentucky. From then on her community was looked after by the two Sulpicians based in Emmitsburg, Frs John Dubois and Simon Bruté, both of whom were helpful and supportive, and very much on her wavelength. In January 1812 the community accepted a rule drawn up for them by Archbishop Carroll, and became the Sisters of Charity of St Joseph. A couple of months later, Elizabeth's daughter Anna died, aged sixteen. Her youngest, Rebecca, was already ailing and would die at fourteen. Both girls had caught TB from their father. Elizabeth was also developing the infection, and she died in 1821 aged only forty-six, but by then the congregation was on its feet. She was canonised in 1975 – the first person born in the USA to be declared a saint.

St Elizabeth Seton, you were called by God to bring up your own children and other people's in the knowledge and love of God. Through your prayers, may he pour out his blessing on all Catholic mothers and teachers, and fill them with wisdom. We ask this through Jesus Christ our Lord. Amen.

St Rose Philippine Duchesne

When the French Revolution broke out in 1798, Rose Philippine Duchesne was living at the Visitandine Convent in Grenoble, where she'd been to school. She wanted to become a nun, but her father had other ideas, and it looked like he'd won when the convent was confiscated by the government and turned into a military barracks and prison. For the next eleven years Philippine lived at home, but refused to get married, and spent her time visiting the poor and sick. During the Terror she took the risk of visiting the political prisoners being held at the former convent to await the guillotine, and like other Catholic women in France at that time, was active in the underground Church. Priests who were faithful to the Pope could only operate in secret, but she knew where to find them, and would fetch them to bring the sacraments to people who were dying. After Napoleon took power and concluded a concordat with the Pope, things started to return to normal. Philippine bought the old convent back, and invited the former nuns to join her there, but by then they were all too aged, and no doubt traumatised, to cope with a return to religious life. In 1804 she gave up on it and joined the Society of the Sacred Heart, a teaching congregation recently founded by Madeleine Sophie Barat. She became a close friend of Mme Barat, and acted as her secretary.

Faraway across the Atlantic, Archbishop Carroll made Fr Louis Dubourg apostolic administrator of Louisiana, and he duly moved to New Orleans, staying at the city's Ursuline Convent, which had been established in imitation of the one in Quebec. But New Orleans had its own way of doing things, and most of the local Catholics could see no reason why they should acknowledge his authority. In 1815 he went to Rome, where he reluctantly agreed to be made a bishop, and return to Louisiana. However he resolved this time to avoid New Orleans, and go instead to Upper Louisiana, where he would be based at St Louis. Before setting off he spent a whole two years in France, recruiting priests and nuns to help him in his own work, and reinforcements for the Ursulines. During his meeting with Mme Barat, whom he'd approached to ask for teaching nuns, Sr Philippine suddenly interrupted the conversation, fell on her knees, and begged to be allowed to go.

Five nuns duly set off in 1818. Sr Philippine, being the eldest at forty-nine, was put in charge though she didn't think she was up to the job. Arriving at St Charles, on the Missouri River, they started their first US convent in a log cabin. Missionary literature about America was heavily focused on the evangelisation of native peoples, but the reality was usually more prosaic. In the years that followed, half a dozen Sacred Heart convents were established in the Mississippi Valley, each running a boarding school, and using the fees to subsidise a free school for poor children. Some of the boarding schools were particularly attractive to rich parents because they were so big and beautifully decorated, but the ones where Rev. Mother Philippine was directly in charge were never so successful. They were plain and dowdy looking, and constantly in debt, because Mother Philippine was always trying to save money to spend on the poor schools, or make donations to the missions working among the native Americans. Besides, she had no talent for being charming to important people. She had never been pretty, and as she grew older she grew uglier and uglier – she was quite frank about it – and even after twenty years in the USA she still couldn't speak English properly. All she could think was that in some mysterious way, God wanted her to serve him through being a total failure in life. She was immensely relieved when at last she was allowed to stop being a superior.

"But she must come too!"

In 1841 Fr Verhaegen, a Belgian Jesuit, arrived at St Charles
to collect four nuns to start a girls' school in eastern Kansas,
for a group of Potawatomi who'd just been moved to a
new location at Sugar Creek. This was as part of the US
government's policy of pushing all the east coast native
American peoples across the Mississippi, to free up their
land for white settlers. However while finalising plans with
the Mother Superior, Fr Verhaegen noticed she was talking
about three nuns, not four. Sr Philippine Duchesne was to
be left behind, because at seventy-one she was too old and
useless. Fr Verhaegen knew that she had dreamed all her
life of being allowed to go and evangelise among the native
Americans, so at once he protested: "But she must come
too! Even if she can use only one leg, she will come. Why,
if we have to carry her all the way on our shoulders, she is
coming with us. She may not be able to do much work, but
she will assure success to the mission by praying for us."

At Sugar Creek Sr Philippine could hardly do anything
to help on a practical level: she couldn't even begin to
learn the Potawatomi language. So she spent most of her
time in the church praying. But the Potawatomi loved
her. They called her Quah-kah-ka-num-ad (Woman-who-
prays-always), and often crept close to touch her habit
so that some of her holiness would rub off on them. Her
health grew steadily worse, and after only two years she

had to return to St Charles. But she continued to pray, and offer up her disappointments and infirmities, for the native American missions until her death in 1852. She was canonised in 1988.

St Philippine Duchesne, God made you a prayerful presence among the marginalised and dispossessed. Through your intercession, help us to trust God to make use of us for his glory, even when we can't see how that could come about. We ask this in Jesus's name. Amen.

Venerable Pierre Toussaint

 Pierre Toussaint was born on a sugar plantation in the French colony of St Domingue. His family were house slaves, highly trusted and well treated. Pierre used to play with the children of Pierre Bérard, the plantation owner after whom he'd been named, and he learned to read and write. When Monsieur and Madame Bérard retired and went to live in Paris, their son Jean-Jacques took over the plantation. Jean-Jacques allowed little Pierre ready access to all the books in the big house, and he read everything he could get his hands on. He was probably about eight when, in 1789, the French Revolution broke out. In St Domingue a civil war blew up between the whites and the mixed race

families, who were not slaves but had no political rights either, and soon afterwards the black slaves, who formed the overwhelming majority of the population, rose in revolt. It was a time of terror and extreme violence, and Pierre saw things that in later life he would refuse – with a shudder – to talk about. After the slaves' final victory, the colony would be renamed Haiti.

Meanwhile, because of the growing tensions and danger, Jean-Jacques decided to take his wife, Marie-Elisabeth, to a safer place until things settled down. The young couple sailed in 1797 for New York, in the newly-independent USA, taking with them a few selected slaves, including Pierre and his little sister Rosalie. Refugees from the revolutions in France and Haiti were flooding into America, many of them destitute, but Jean-Jacques had brought a considerable amount of money with him to be invested in New York, so as to assure his wife a secure income and a comfortably high standard of living. He decided Pierre should learn hairdressing, and apprenticed him to a hairdresser shortly before returning alone to St Domingue, in a bid to protect the family plantation from confiscation. A letter arrived for Marie-Elisabeth to tell her he'd failed, and was returning to the US, but then came another letter saying he'd suddenly been taken ill, and was dead.

Shortly after this, the New York firm in which he'd invested his money went bankrupt: Marie-Elisabeth was left with nothing. She got together her jewellery and told Pierre to sell it to pay her debts. Instead Pierre lent her all his savings, and from then on he quietly and unobtrusively made himself responsible for the household finances. He knew only too well that if Marie-Elisabeth could not pay her way, her creditors would seize what assets she had, including her slaves: he and Rosalie would be sold at auction. He'd become such a talented hairdresser that he was earning good money, particularly as the Bérard's high-society connections helped him build up a network of fashionable and wealthy New Yorkers, but he had to work very, very hard to make ends meet.

Marie-Elisabeth died in 1807, setting Pierre free on her deathbed. He then set himself to saving money to buy the liberty of Rosalie, and of another girl called Juliette Noel. It took him four years – during which he also donated generously to other good causes, such as the building fund for St Patrick's Cathedral – but he did it. In 1811 Rosalie married Jean Noel, a relative of Juliette's, and three months later Pierre married Juliette. Both weddings were celebrated at St Peter's. Pierre and Juliette made a very happy couple, though they were saddened by their inability to have children. Rosalie's marriage was not happy: Jean did a runner, leaving her pregnant, so she went to live with Pierre and Juliette, and when she died of TB in 1816, they adopted her baby daughter Euphémie.

An exemplary couple

Pierre and Juliette believed in enjoying, and sharing, the good things of life, and they always had time for their friends and for people in need. They took in lodgers, sometimes for the money but often to help out people who couldn't pay: sick priests, or orphaned boys. Pierre spent very little on himself, but whenever he heard of a whip round for someone in trouble he immediately put his hand in his pocket. Besides financial help, all kinds of people – French or American, black or white – knew they could always call on him for good advice, both practical and spiritual, and he acted as a clearing house of useful information – putting refugees in touch with organisations that might help them, or finding them pupils so they could support themselves by giving French lessons. His hairdressing clients used to confide their worries to him, knowing he could be relied on not to gossip; they also gave him donations for his charities, and he always kept careful accounts. When yellow fever epidemics broke out during hot summers in the crowded, insanitary city, he rescued and nursed sick people who'd been abandoned with nobody to look after them. Although he gave a lot of money away, Pierre also invested wisely, in real estate and insurance companies, and became quite rich. For sixty years he attended the daily morning six o'clock Mass at St Peter's, and he belonged to the parish's Benevolent Society, which raised and distributed funds for the poor. When Mother

Elizabeth Seton sent Sisters from Emmitsburg to open a Catholic orphanage, he became one of their most valued and most faithful supporters and fundraisers. Juliette was a lifelong supporter of the Oblate Sisters of Providence, a black congregation started in Baltimore by Mother Mary Lange.

Sadly Euphémie, like her mother, had TB, and to Pierre's profound grief she died in 1829, aged fourteen. By 1835 he was planning to retire to France, to spend his old age in peace away from the rampant racism and anti-Catholicism in New York. But just then New York suffered a disastrous fire, which bankrupted the insurance companies he'd invested in, and he lost most of his money. His friends offered to help, but he said no, he could manage, and other people were in more need than he was. He continued working, walking from one hairdressing appointment to another. A white friend thoughtlessly asked him why he didn't take an omnibus, but black people weren't allowed on public transport. In August 1842 he and Juliette attended a special service at St Patrick's Cathedral, but were thrown out by an usher who said no black people were allowed in. The president of the cathedral trustees, a personal friend of Pierre's, was shocked when he heard, and wrote to apologise. But even within the Church, racist practices were routine and rarely challenged.

Juliette died in 1851, and Pierre in 1853. They were buried together, in the same grave as Euphémie, in the churchyard of St Patrick's – the old cathedral, not the present building on Fifth Avenue. In 1991, after a cause had been opened for Pierre's canonisation, his body was exhumed and reburied in the crypt of the new St Patrick's Cathedral, among the tombs of the archbishops. After careful investigation, his heroic virtues were recognised by the Church in 1996.

Lord God our Father, help us to learn from Ven. Pierre Toussaint to find peace in knowing that our worth and dignity comes from you, regardless of how others treat us. If it is your will, may he be counted among your saints, for the glory of your name, through Jesus Christ our Lord. Amen.

The Melting Pot that Wasn't

The middle decades of the nineteenth century saw millions migrating from Europe to the US, mostly from Ireland and from the German-speaking areas of Central Europe, in search of a better life. Many of them were Catholics, and they had to face furious anti-Catholic and anti-immigrant hostility and violence. In New York the Irish fought to defend St Patrick's against attacks by the "Know Nothing" Movement, and Know Nothing rioters in Philadelphia burned down several churches. Human nature being what it is, once the earlier waves of immigrants became established, they sought to bolster their new American identities by discriminating against more recently arrived ethnic groups. Moreover most of the European immigrants, anxious to share the privileges of whiteness, were all too ready to collude with white racism against black people.

St John Nepomucene Neumann

John Neumann was born in 1811 in Bohemia (Czech Republic). His father was Bavarian and his mother Czech, and he grew up speaking Czech, with German a close second; he was proud to have been given the baptismal name John Nepomucene

"in honour of the glorious Patron of Bohemia." He chose to study for the priesthood, though the atmosphere in the seminary made him quite miserable: some of the teachers belonged to a movement which wanted to downplay papal authority and allow the Church to be controlled by national governments, and treated any kind of serious spirituality as a waste of time and money. It was a breath of fresh air for him to read in a missionary magazine about the work of the Slovene priest Fr Frederic Baraga, who'd escaped from that kind of atmosphere by going to the US to work among the Ottawa and Chippewa peoples.

Young Neumann decided to follow Fr Baraga's example and go to America. His bishop made no objection, but nor did he offer any assistance or even write him a letter of recommendation. In 1836 John set off anyway for Le Havre, walking much of the way to save money, and bought the cheapest passage he could find across the Atlantic. His letters hadn't been answered, so he had no idea what reception he would get, but within three weeks of landing in New York he had been ordained, and appointed to look after German immigrants in the Niagara Falls area, scattered over a "parish" covering nine hundred square miles. At first he walked from place, carrying his Mass kit in a rucksack. On one occasion he was so tired, he fainted in the woods, and was found and rescued by native Americans. After that someone gave him a horse, but people laughed at him because he was so short, his feet didn't reach the stirrups. He already spoke seven major languages and a number of Slav dialects, and when he discovered that some of the Irish in America could not speak English, he learned Gaelic too. But although he was very dedicated to his pastoral work, he found the isolation very difficult to cope with, and it made him think seriously about the need to be part of a priestly community.

In 1840 Neumann arranged to join the Redemptorists, and was sent to Pittsburgh, a growing industrial city with large numbers of German immigrants working in its steel mills. The Redemptorists were based at the "factory church", a former cotton factory where they said Mass for a German congregation, and they also served several outlying Mass centres. After completing his novitiate and making his vows in Baltimore, Fr Neumann was sent back to Pittsburgh in 1844 as parish priest and superior, with Fr Francis Xavier Seelos, from Bavaria, assigned as curate. Their makeshift clergy house, where the rain sometimes came through the roof, was so small that they had to share a room, partitioned by a curtain down the middle. Fr Seelos never forgot what a help Fr Neumann had been to him as a young priest, in terms of both spiritual advice and mentoring, and practical kindness. Fr Neumann seemed to sleep very little, and spend most of the night praying, and early each morning he got up first and lit a fire, to take the chill off for when Fr Seelos got up. He also insisted on taking all the night sick calls. After completing the building of a proper church,

St Philomena's, to replace the old factory, Fr Neumann set about constructing a decent residence. In 1847 he was made superior of all the Redemptorists in the USA, and in 1848 he became a naturalised US citizen.

Bishop of Philadelphia

When Fr Neumann was made Bishop of Philadelphia, in 1852, some people were delighted – such as the Irish grandmother who, after making her confession to him in Gaelic, went round telling everyone how marvellous it was that Philadelphia had once again been given an Irish bishop! However not everyone was pleased. There were those who thought the post should have gone to someone more impressive, who knew how to talk to important people and get money out of them. Fr Neumann had an accent, always dressed shabbily, never tried to impress anyone and was much happier among the poor than the rich. Besides, he did not want to be a bishop, and only agreed when the Pope sent him a direct order. One of the first things he did was to introduce the Forty Hours Devotion – the prolonged exposition of the Blessed Sacrament, with the church sanctuary beautifully decorated with candles and flowers, and relays of people coming to pray day and night. There'd been a fear of holding such an event, for fear of attack and profanation by the Know Nothings, but Bishop Neumann resolved to trust God, went ahead, and organised it throughout the diocese.

The Catholic population in and around Philadelphia was already very high, and growing fast, mainly due to immigration, so more churches were urgently needed: during his time as bishop he was to open nearly eighty new ones. At the same time he had to struggle against laypeople who were trying to wrest control of their parishes from the clergy in the name of "democracy" (which in practice was liable to mean everything being run by a small clique in their own interests). All the new churches, and his determination that every parish in the diocese should have its own school, meant he was soon up to his ears in debt. Kind people started to say the dear bishop was a holy man, but hopelessly incompetent. He never defended himself against the gossip. On 5th January 1860 he felt a little unwell, but said he was sure he'd feel better after a walk in the fresh air. For no apparent reason he added, "A man must always be ready, for death comes when and where God wills it." A few hours later he collapsed in the street, and was taken into a nearby house, but was dead before a priest could arrive to give him the last rites. He was canonised in 1977.

St John Neumann, pray for us to God that our love for the Holy Eucharist may be ever deepened, and that we may always be ready for death. We ask this through Jesus Christ our Lord. Amen.

Venerable Henriette Delille

The slave who came to be known as Nanette Dubreuil was landed in New Orleans in the 1720s. Probably a Wolof from Senegal or Gambia, she was purchased by the Dubreuil family as a domestic worker. In 1730 a women's confraternity, the Children of Mary, was formed in New Orleans with the help of the Ursulines, to evangelise the slaves. The Dubreil womenfolk all joined, and it wasn't long before Nanette was a baptised and practising Catholic, busy catechising other slaves. Claude Joseph Dubreuil, head of the family, took a different kind of interest in Nanette, making her his mistress. Everyone understood that Nanette had very little choice, and nobody blamed her. After his death the Dubreuil family eventually freed Nanette, her children and her grandchildren.

When the US flag was first raised over New Orleans, it had a population of perhaps ten thousand, and a very different social set up from what prevailed in most of the USA: predominantly French-speaking and Catholic, and a mixture of whites, "free people of colour", and black slaves. This pattern was reinforced by the influx in 1809 of around nine thousand French-speaking refugees from Haiti, comprising roughly equal numbers of whites, free blacks, and enslaved blacks belonging to the first two groups. US whites moving into Louisiana thought New Orleans society very odd, and it made them quite uncomfortable to see black and mixed-race people who were free, wealthy and assertive.

Nanette's great great granddaughters, Cecilia and Henriette Delille, were extraordinarily beautiful and accomplished young women. Their mother had been careful to teach her daughters all the social graces: deportment, dancing and dress sense, knowledge of French literature and music, and also some practical skills like home nursing which were considered especially useful for women of their class. In the male line their ancestry was white all the way back to Dubreuil, and they were so light-skinned they could easily pass as white themselves. The family tradition was for the women in each generation to find a white protector with plenty of money to keep them in style. It never involved marriage: interracial marriage was illegal. Nevertheless the arrangement was a time-honoured New Orleans custom, known as plaçage. When Cecilia was seventeen, she made her mother very happy by entering into a highly satisfactory plaçage relationship with a wealthy Austrian merchant.

Choosing Christ

The Ursulines had a long tradition of providing education for all three racial groups – white girls, free girls of colour, and black slave girls. At their request Bishop Dubourg had brought Sr Marthe Fontière, a Hospitaller nun, from France to New Orleans to take over their school for free girls of colour, because the Ursulines needed to move to a new convent in a different part of the city. It charged fees of between $1.50 and $5 a month, and had about eighty girls enrolled – among them Henriette. In the evenings the school was used as a catechetical centre for adults, and Sr Marthe encouraged the older students to help with the catechesis. In 1827 Henriette, aged fourteen, joined the little group of enthusiastic teenagers who were busy visiting black people who were poor, old or sick, giving religious instruction to slaves on the nearby plantations, and meeting for prayer in the Ursuline Convent. She loved it, and decided this was what she wanted for her life.

Henriette's family were horrified. Not only had she rejected the plaçage for which her expensive upbringing had prepared her, but she was actually planning a course in life which would identify her publicly with the poor black underclass from whom they were trying so hard to distance themselves. Her mother had a nervous breakdown, but nothing could deter Henriette. In 1836 she wrote a resolution on the flypage of her prayer book: "I believe in God. I hope in God. I love. I want to live and die for God." Accordingly she sold her inheritance, and organised a lay community, the Sisters of the Presentation, to care for the sick, help the poor, and instruct the ignorant.

This community struggled for a while before breaking up under the pressure of public opinion. Some of the girls immigrated to France, where race restrictions were less rigid, and entered convents there. But Henriette and her friend, Juliette Gaudin, were determined to start a community in New Orleans. Meanwhile they continued their social and catechetical work as laywomen.

With permission from Bishop Antoine Blanc, and with the solid support of Fr Étienne Rousselon, they collected money to rent a house, and in 1842 founded the Sisters of the Holy Family with just three members: Henriette as superior, Juliette Gaudin and Josephine Charles. They took in elderly women with nowhere else to go. The first few years were a time of poverty, ridicule, harassment and apparent failure. They received all kinds of donations – small sums of money, food, a little coffee or a wheelbarrow full of firewood – but they often used to go to bed hungry, praying that someone would knock on the door and offer them something, if only a little sugar to ease the hunger pangs. They had to be careful not to draw too much attention to what they were doing, so they did not wear habits but only plain blue percale dresses, with black bonnets, and they avoided publicity. Henriette went to do a novitiate with the Sisters of the Sacred Heart, and passed on what she'd learned to her two companions. With time they were able to establish a boarding school for free girls of colour, which brought in a small but steady income. Teaching slaves to read and write had been made illegal, but they continued to run religious instruction classes for the slaves, both children and adults. They also encouraged and helped slaves who wanted to get properly married in church.

When the American Civil War broke out, Louisiana voted for secession, and New Orleans played a vital role in supplying troops, weapons and other supplies to the Confederate forces. This made it a target, and in the spring of 1862 it was occupied by Union troops. On 22nd September, after the Battle of Antietam, Abraham Lincoln issued the Emancipation Proclamation, making the abolition of slavery in the US an official war aim. Henriette Delille died on 16th November 1862, aged only forty-nine, having worn herself out through hard work for the poorest of her people. In 2004 the Sisters of the Holy Family opened a cause for her canonisation, and her heroic virtues were recognised in 2010.

God our Father, through the example of Ven. Henriette Delille who refused to sell her body for a life of luxury, help us to uphold and defend Christian marriage. We ask that, if it is your will, she may be counted among your saints, for the glory of your name, through Jesus Christ our Lord. Amen.

St Francesca Cabrini

Mass immigration from Italy to the USA began to develop during the 1870s, and took off in the 1880s. "Little Italies" developed in major US cities, where Italian immigrants lived crowded together in great poverty, and where the English language was never heard. It was difficult for the Italians to relate to the Catholic Church in America, or to any of its social institutions, because of the language and cultural barriers. They were notorious for hardly ever being seen at Mass, their children were rarely to be found in Catholic schools, and they were contemptuously dismissed as "bad Catholics", not worth the time and trouble of trying to reach out to. Protestant charities *were* reaching out to them, offering practical help, but usually with ulterior motives of proselytisation. A common practice was to offer to take care of children when a family couldn't cope – usually because one parent was ill, or had died. The children were whisked away to a distant orphanage, too far for visits, and eventually given up for adoption by a Protestant family. Bishop Scalabrini of Piacenza, who was deeply concerned about the migrants, sent priests out to the US to work with the Italians there. He also wanted to send women religious, and the Missionary Sisters of the Sacred Heart, a new and vigorous little congregation, struck him as ideal.

Born in 1850 into a large farming family in Sant'Angelo Lodigiano, northern Italy, Francesca Cabrini had qualified as a schoolteacher before starting that congregation. She'd insisted on having "missionary" in the name, despite widespread objections that only men could be missionaries: Italian dictionaries didn't even list the word in the feminine form. (They do now!) She kept abreast of all the latest ideas in education, and had a flair for getting things done. Bishop Scalabrini arranged for her to be sent a personal invitation from Archbishop Corrigan of New York, but her dream was to be a missionary in China. However he wouldn't give up, and she began to come round. She went to Rome, explained the whole situation honestly to Pope Leo XIII, and agreed to let him decide. He told her: "Go west, not east!" and she obeyed, setting off for New York with six Sisters.

They received a warm welcome from the Scalabrini Fathers, but the house they'd been told was waiting for them didn't exist. They had to book into lodgings at the Chinatown end of Manhattan's Little Italy, sitting up all night on hard chairs because the beds were full of bugs. Then it turned out the archbishop had changed his mind: he wanted them to turn round and go straight home. Mother Cabrini stood her ground and said the Pope had sent them, so they'd better stay. Backing down, the archbishop took them to stay with the Sisters of Charity until they could find a place of their own. Within a few months Mother Cabrini had got both a school and an orphanage up and running.

The reason for Archbishop Corrigan's strange behaviour was that he'd been got at by anti-immigrant Catholics, and this scenario was to repeat itself again and again. US Catholicism might be a minority religion, but it was well organised and rapidly throwing up new churches, schools, orphanages and hospitals to serve its fast-expanding numbers. However the richest and most powerful Catholics were of Irish or German descent, desperate to become fully assimilated into American society, and very anxious to downplay anything that got them stigmatised as "different". They did not want to help Italians, whom they saw as a liability and an embarrassment, to feel more at home in "their Church", and they also wanted any money available to be ring fenced for their own projects, not spent on "dirty Italians". Any bishop who tried to help the Italians was liable to face a campaign of pressure and harassment to force him to back off. Moreover the Italian immigrants themselves were so riven with factional disputes, it was almost impossible to get them to co-operate on anything.

Missionary journeys

Mother Cabrini couldn't speak much English at first, and of course she had no money. She visited Italian patients in the public hospitals who were dying alone, and without the sacraments, because none of the staff spoke Italian. She hated the idea of moving into healthcare, but then she had a dream in which she saw Our Lady, with her sleeves rolled up, busy making hospital beds and saying, "I am doing what you refuse to do." So she started her own hospital in New York. Archbishop Corrigan donated fifty dollars, and four well-off Italians gave fifty dollars each. Two hundred and fifty dollars was enough to rent a building for a month and install ten cheap beds: the Sisters slept on the floor. Nevertheless the project took off, and Mother Cabrini subsequently opened a second hospital in Chicago. Both hospitals were named after Christopher Columbus – the only famous Italian that all Italians could agree to admire.

During her lifetime Mother Cabrini made repeated trips across the Atlantic, and travelled widely across America by train or on muleback, setting up a string of Italian schools, orphanages and hostels in major cities across the USA. She also established houses in a number of other countries, mostly in Latin America, but also in France and Spain. She and her Sisters were active in parishes, running catechetical programmes and sodalities, and they visited prisoners, especially those on Death Row in Sing Sing. In Denver, where they had a large orphanage to care for children orphaned through mining accidents, they used to go down the mines themselves to evangelise the Italian workers there. In 1909 Mother Cabrini became a naturalised US citizen.

Around the turn of the century Mother Cabrini had begun to think about making a foundation in London, to help the congregation recruit more English-speaking Sisters, who were desperately needed to staff schools in the US. With the agreement of Francis Bourne, then Bishop of Southwark and later Archbishop of Westminster, she opened a convent and boarding school in Brockley, which later moved to Honor Oak. For her ninth missionary journey, in 1912, the London Sisters wanted to give her a treat, so they booked her on a new state-of-the-art luxury passenger liner. However she decided to leave earlier than planned, and the Titanic sailed without her. She was still in the US on 4th July 1914, when the Sisters there held a big celebration to mark the twenty-fifth anniversary of their arrival in New York. The outbreak of the First World War then made it inadvisable to return to Europe. Mother Francesca Cabrini died in her Chicago hospital on 22nd December 1917. She was canonised in 1946, and is the patron saint of migrants. In 2009 a shrine in her honour was inaugurated for the UK, at Southwark Cathedral.

St Francesca Cabrini, you crossed oceans and continents to defend the dignity of migrants and help them integrate into new cultures: pray for us, that we may receive grace to welcome migrants and recognise our common humanity. We ask this through Jesus Christ our Lord. Amen.

St Katharine Drexel

 Elizabeth, Katharine and Louise Drexel grew up together in a happy Catholic home in Philadelphia. Their wealthy parents were very generous supporters of all kinds of good causes, and they helped their mother with her charity work which, always after careful investigation, gave about thirty thousand dollars every year to people in need. In 1870 they acquired a summer holiday home in the Pennsylvania countryside, which they called St Michel. Elizabeth was then fourteen, and Katharine eleven, and they started a Sunday school there for the servants' and neighbours' children. During the winter the girls also helped out with a Sunday school for black children at Old St Joseph's, the oldest Catholic church in Philadelphia. Bishop Neumann's successor, Bishop Woods, was a friend of the family, and after he had given them permission to have Mass in the little chapel, Fr James O'Connor, the local parish priest, became a frequent visitor. In 1876, when Katharine was eighteen, Fr O'Connor was made Vicar Apostolic of Nebraska, a vast and wild missionary territory. The family often used to receive letters from him about the native Americans, who had been driven onto reservations where they were living in wretched poverty. Many were Catholics, and Bishop O'Connor was keen

to establish schools for them, so they could get a good education and establish themselves better in US society. The Drexels were very generous in their donations for his work, along with all their other good causes.

In 1885 their father died, and the three sisters inherited fourteen million dollars between them. Shortly afterwards they made a trip to Europe, during which they had a private audience with Pope Leo XIII. They asked him to send more missionaries to help the native Americans in the US, but the Pope asked Katharine, "My child, why not become a missionary yourself?" Katharine had, in fact, been thinking very seriously about becoming a nun, though Bishop O'Connor, who was her spiritual advisor, was against the idea.

In 1887, after sailing back across the Atlantic, the Drexel sisters made a trip out to the Indian Territories to see conditions for themselves, assess the work of the schools and other mission projects they'd been supporting, and consult native American leaders. Deeply impressed, they made a second trip the following year, and continued to found schools for native Americans all over the US. At the same time they were beginning to realise that despite the abolition of slavery, African Americans were still denied proper educational facilities and civil rights, especially in the old south. They became determined to find a way of giving them, too, the means to break the bonds of oppression.

Sisters of the Blessed Sacrament

When it became clear to Katharine that no existing religious congregation was dedicated to carrying out the mission to which she believed God was calling her, she resolved to found a new one: the Sisters of the Blessed Sacrament. In 1889, she arranged to do a novitiate in an established convent, choosing the Sisters of Mercy because of her devotion to the Eucharist: they were allowed daily Communion, at a time when most congregations only allowed Communion a few times a week. Elizabeth had died tragically young, so her share had been divided between the other two, and Katharine now had seven million dollars. In 1892 she and thirteen companions moved into a house in Bensalem, Pennsylvania: this was to be their first convent, and it had a boarding school for black children attached. The USA's two struggling black congregations, the Sisters of the Holy Family, and the Oblate Sisters of Providence, specifically asked her not to recruit African Americans, but direct any black applicants their way, so she did as they asked, while also supporting them financially. The Sisters of the Blessed Sacrament did, however, accept native American candidates. Mother Francesca Cabrini advised Katharine to take the rule she'd drawn up for her congregation to Rome for approval, and Pope Pius X granted preliminary approval in 1907.

Some of Mother Katharine's money was used to fund the work of her own congregation, but she continued to give most of it away to other organisations and projects with similar aims. Before the Civil War a significant proportion of the black slaves in the south had been Catholics, but the Church had failed to look after them properly, and they had dropped away. All institutions in America were segregated, and the Catholic churches were no different: black people had to sit on a few benches set aside for them at the back. Mother Katharine did not think she could manage to end segregation, but at least she could even things up a bit. She never forgot the Golden Rule: whoever has the gold makes the rules. So she began negotiating with the bishops, providing money to build schools for black Catholics. She also offered money for churches, with one special condition: in every church built with her money a whole aisle, from the front to the back, had to be reserved for black worshippers. Naturally there was opposition: in 1922 the Ku Klux Klan in Texas threatened to dynamite one of the Sisters' mission churches, and tar and feather the parish priest. The Sisters prayed about it, and a few days later the Klan's local headquarters was struck by a tornado. Occasionally Mother Katharine gave public talks: the Drexel name would draw a sizeable audience of respectable white Catholics who were then most surprised to hear this nun, in her quiet voice, telling them home truths about racism within the Church – and the hypocrisy of making donations to charity while upholding structural injustice. In 1932 she founded Xavier University, the first Catholic university for African Americans, in New Orleans.

A few years later Mother Katharine's health failed, forcing her to make a radical change of lifestyle. Her last twenty years were spent happily praying in her room, with occasional outings in a wheelchair. She died in 1955 at the age of ninety-seven, and was canonised in 2000 by Pope John Paul II.

St Katharine Drexel, you were raised up by God to work for the rights of the poor and oppressed. Through your prayers, and through participation in the Eucharistic Communion of his Church, may we be drawn to share your thirst for justice. We ask this through Jesus Christ our Lord. Amen.

Two Nations under God

Both the US and Canada developed into federal countries stretching across vast expanses of North America from the Atlantic to the Pacific: the boundary between them is the world's largest international frontier. But it doesn't matter how large your country is, or how small: we all of us need holy men and women to remind us what really matters, and point us towards eternal life.

St André Bessette

In 1870 Alfred Bessette, a twenty-five year-old unskilled labourer recently returned to Canada after a few years as a migrant factory worker in the USA, applied to join the Congregation of the Holy Cross. The Brothers were rather embarrassed. He had such a strong recommendation from his parish priest, Fr André Provençal, that they didn't like to turn him down flat. But they were a teaching order, and Alfred could barely sign his name. The eighth of twelve children born into a poor working-class family, he'd been baptised as soon as he was born, for fear he wouldn't survive. He'd then lost both his parents by the age of twelve, and had hardly any schooling. Nevertheless the Brothers agreed to find him a place at Notre Dame College, a boys' boarding school on the edge of Montreal, as porter and general odd-job-man. On 27th December 1870 he was clothed in the Holy Cross habit, and renamed in honour of his sponsor, becoming Brother André (Andrew). Only a few weeks previously, Pope Pius IX had issued a decree declaring St Joseph patron of the Universal Church, and Brother André was to develop a great devotion to St Joseph.

Although he seemed frail, Brother André was originally from a farming community and had been used to working hard all his life up to then. One of the problems facing him as a Brother was that there wasn't enough real serious work around the school that he was considered capable of. All his spare energy went into prayer: he often spent the whole night praying. Sometimes when he had no work to do, he would slip across the street to wander around Mount Royal, and scatter holy medals on the hillside. If anyone asked, he said it was to get St Joseph's help to enable the congregation to buy the land, and build a chapel there. The boys in the school made fun of his simple piety, and the other Brothers looked down on him as a bit of a liability.

Increasingly, however, people were coming to Notre Dame specifically to talk to Brother André. He was someone to whom they could tell their troubles, and they began asking him to pray for them when they were ill. Brother André would pray with them, and give them a medal of St Joseph and a few drops of olive oil from the lamp burning before his statue in the chapel. When cures began to be reported, Brother André gave all the credit to St Joseph, but inevitably word began to spread that the little doorkeeper could perform miracles. Every day crowds of visitors, many of them looking extremely ill, would be waiting in the school foyer to see him and ask for his prayers. Parents started to complain. The Brothers felt they were being made a laughing stock. The Archbishop of Montreal asked the Holy Cross Superior: "Would he stop seeing the sick if you asked him? Would Brother André obey?" "Immediately, your Lordship," was the reply. "Well, in that case, let him be. If the work is of God, it will continue. If it is not, it will cease." Eventually the Brothers made him set up an office across the street, at the tram stop, and see his patients there.

Montreal was growing fast. Worried that their posh college might be boxed in all round and lose its social cachet, the Holy Cross Brothers decided in 1896 to purchase the hillside opposite Notre Dame. Brother André started building. He had no money except two hundred dollars he had saved from the tips he earned giving haircuts to the boys, but he had a lot of willing friends to help him. The first little chapel to St Joseph was blessed in 1904. Brother André, at the age of sixty, left Notre Dame and moved into a little loft at the back of the chapel to act as caretaker. The crowds coming to pray in the chapel grew larger and larger each year, and eventually the Holy Cross Brothers decided to co-operate with the project: this made it much easier to raise funds, and in 1924 the foundations were laid for a huge basilica. Brother André saw the roof go on before he died, on 6th January 1937, aged ninety-two – quite an achievement for a baby not expected to live! St Joseph's Oratory was finally completed only in 1967, but is now Montreal's most famous landmark: two million people visit and pray there each year. It is also the largest shrine in the world dedicated to St Joseph. Brother André was canonised in 2010.

St André Bessette, you served God all your life in humility and simplicity. Pray for us, that we may learn from St Joseph, and from you, what it is like to be close to Jesus and do his work in the world. Amen.

Blessed Carlos Manuel Rodríguez Santiago

Puerto Rico had been a Spanish colony since the time of Columbus, and most Puerto Ricans are of Spanish descent and Spanish-speaking. But they are also US citizens, because the island became a territory of the USA in 1898. Carlos Rodríguez was born in Cagua, Puerto Rico, in November 1918 shortly after the end of the First World War. When he was six, his father's little shop next to the house caught fire, and the family lost their shop, their home and everything they had. They all went to live with Carlos's grandmother, who was a very devout Catholic, and had a strong influence on the spiritual development of Carlos, his three sisters and his brother.

Carlos was very clever and very interested in everything, and did well at school – always top of the class, and acquiring an excellent command of English. He loved classical music, and taught himself to play the piano beautifully after only a few formal lessons. As a teenager, he saved up to buy a bilingual missal for his little sisters, but because missals with Spanish translations of the Latin text were very expensive, and he only had thirty-five cents, he bought one with an English translation. It turned out the girls' English wasn't up to it, so he had to explain to them what it said, but his explanations brought the meaning of the Mass to life both for him and them, much more vividly than if they'd just read the translation. However Carlos's education was disrupted when he developed a medical condition, ulcerative colitis. As far as the family could work out, it was triggered by stress, due to a hair-raising incident when he defended a baby cousin from a neighbour's vicious dog that got loose and ran into their house. Whenever it flared up he had to miss classes, and because of his recurrent illnesses, he didn't finish high school till 1939, when he was twenty-one.

Rejected by the army on medical grounds, Carlos spent the Second World War doing secretarial work at the Camp O'Reilly army base on Puerto Rico. In 1946 he enrolled at the University of Puerto Rico, where he made lots of friends to whom he was known as "Charlie", but once again his illness got in the way, and after a year he dropped out. For the rest of his life he worked as a clerk at the Agricultural Experiment Station, translating English documents into Spanish. Although he'd abandoned formal studies, he carried on reading books and learning new things. In particular he read books that could help him go deeper into the meaning of the Christian faith, and he was thrilled by the new ideas which were emerging around that time, pointing towards the liturgical and spiritual renewal which would be called for by Vatican II.

"We live for that night!"

As well as attending daily Mass, and setting aside times for prayer and for spiritual reading, Carlos began to develop an apostolate among the laypeople of his home parish and the university students. Being passionate about the importance of meaningful participation in the liturgy, he organised liturgy circles. He also held "Days of Christian Living" for small groups: they'd bring food for a shared lunch, there'd be prayer times and games, and Carlos gave talks which made a life-changing impact on those who heard them, although he was quite shy and didn't see himself as a public speaker. Occasionally these Days would be organised ecumenically, with non-Catholics invited to join in. Carlos spent his lunch hours typing up little newsletters, often comprising useful articles that he'd translated: he'd mimeograph them and post them out, spending quite a lot of his salary on stationery and stamps. He believed very strongly that the Church should allow the Mass to be celebrated in the vernacular, because he knew that even quite well-educated Catholics couldn't follow the meaning of the Latin. In 1952 came a very important liturgical reform, aimed at restoring the Easter Vigil to what it had been in the Early Church, as the highpoint of the Christian year. For centuries it had been observed on Easter Saturday morning, but Pope Pius XII moved it back to the night, so it really became the Vigil of the Resurrection leading into Easter Sunday. Carlos threw himself into helping everyone understand what a marvellous gift this was: he used to say, "We live for that night!"

In March 1963 Carlos had an operation, during which the doctors discovered cancer. He spent the next few months helpless and bedbound, in a lot of pain and discomfort, and acutely embarrassed about having been given a colostomy. Although he'd always been a very joyful person, he went through a really bad patch, thinking God had abandoned him. At Easter his friends brought him a candle lit from the Paschal Candle. He was too ill to attend his brother Pepe's ordination as a Benedictine priest, but managed to watch his first Mass from a wheelchair in the sacristy. Only towards the end of the second week in July did Carlos regain his peace. His family spent the day on 12th July praying and singing with him. Shortly after midnight Pepe sang the Easter Exultet: "This is the night when Jesus Christ broke the chains of death and rose triumphant from the grave!" Just as he finished, Carlos died. Afterwards the family was going to sell a piece of land, the only property Carlos owned, to pay his medical bills, but the doctors told them not to worry, saying: "We owe Charlie far more than he owes us." Carlos Rodríguez was beatified in 2001.

Bl. Carlos Rodríguez, we ask your prayers that we may enter ever more deeply into the liturgy – the work of the people of God – above all on that night which saw the glorious Resurrection of our Lord Jesus Christ, who lives and reigns with the Father and the Holy Spirit, for ever and ever. Amen.

Afterword

Such a short booklet can be no more than an introduction to the saints of North America. If it's caught your interest, do try to find out more. It's necessarily had to be selective, and not everyone will agree with the selection. It wasn't possible even to include all the canonised and beatified figures – among them St John Neumann's curate, Fr Francis Seelos, who was beatified in 2000, or Fr Stanley Rother, the Oklahoma farm boy martyred in Guatemala in 1981, whose beatification is expected in 2017 – or so much as look at the saints of Mexico. The full list of people who were important for the Catholic history of the US and Canada, and for whom causes have been opened or proposed, is long and fascinating: it includes Frs Eusebio Kino and Fr Frederic Baraga, who've been mentioned here, but it also includes Dorothy Day and Fulton Sheen (on whom CTS booklets are available); Fr Augustine Tolton, the first black US priest; Sr Blandina Segale, who took on Billy the Kid; Catherine de Hueck Doherty; Georges and Pauline Vanier; and many, many more. Books and articles, ranging from cosy little hagiographic accounts and historical novels to huge scholarly tomes, are readily available in English about the saints of North America, and CTS has a booklet on St Damien de Veuster. It's also very easy to find information about North American saints on the internet. You can make a virtual pilgrimage to their shrines and the places where they lived. You can read the *Jesuit Relations* online. You can play St Jean de Brébeuf's *Huron Carol* on Wikipedia, or "Vivimos para esa Noche" ("We Live for that Night"), the song written by Norma T Diaz Camacho for Carlos Rodriguez's beatification ceremony, on YouTube. Films have been made about a lot of the North American saints, and some are obtainable on DVD or accessible online. Material about St André Bessette is readily available on the Salt+Light Media website, and a documentary film about St Marie de l'Incarnation – *Madwoman of God* – can be viewed online courtesy of the National Film Council of Canada: *https://www.nfb.ca/film/madwoman_of_god/* (French with English subtitles). For details of Serra Clubs in England and Scotland, e-mail: *foundation@serragb. org.uk*

Image Credits

Page 7: *Portrait of Mother Mary of the Incarnation*, Archives of the Ursulines of Quebec, public domain; page 15: *North American Martyrs* © Wikimedia Commons; page 15: *Le Venerable Marguerite Bourgeoys* © Wikimedia Commons; page 18: *François de Montmorency-Laval* from The Project Gutenberg EBook of Canada, J. G. Bourinot, 1897. In that book's list of illustrations, this illustration is noted as reproduced from Sulte's *Histoire des Canadiens-Français*, public domain; page 23: *Saint Kateri Tekakwitha* by Fr Claude Chauchetière around 1696, © Wikimedia Commons; page 35: *Junípero Serra*, copyright unknown. Page 41: *Saint Elizabeth Ann Seton* © Wikimedia Commons; page 47: *St Rose Duchesne*, copyright unknown. Page 51: *Pierre Toussaint* © Wikimedia Commons; page 57: *Saint John Neumann* © Wikimedia Commons; page 62: *Henriette Delille*, copyright unknown. Page 67: *Saint Francesca Xavier Cabrini* © Wikimedia Commons; page 72: *St Katharine Drexel* © Wikimedia Commons; page 77: *Saint André Bessette* © Wikimedia Commons; page 80: *Carlos Manuel Rodríguez Santiago* © Wikimedia Commons. Every effort has been made to trace the copyright holders. The publisher would be grateful to receive any further information.

Saints of Africa

Jean Olwen Maynard

The African saints that Catholics are most likely to have heard of - even if they don't know much about them - lived a very long time ago, and often in parts of Africa which are no longer Christian. In our own time, and in the more recently Christianised parts of Africa, the Catholic Church is growing faster than perhaps anywhere else in the world - but what do we know about the modern saints of Africa such as Daudi Okelo, Clementine Anuarite, Ghebre-Michael, Victoria Rasoamanarivo, to name a few? Here's a chance to find out.

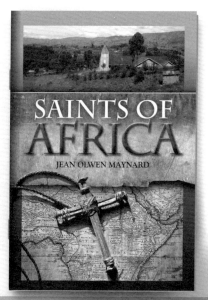

B762   ISBN 978 1 78469 037 3